CEPHALOPODIC
WINNER OF THE 2014 KITHARA BOOK PRIZE

CEPHALOPODIC

AND OTHER OTHERLY LOVE POEMS BY
J.P. DANCING BEAR

Copyright © 2015 J.P. Dancing Bear
Paperback ISBN: 978-1-941783-06-1

All rights reserved: except for the purpose of quoting brief passages for review, no part of this book may be reproduced or transmitted in any form or by any means, electronic or mechanical, including photocopying, recording, or by any information storage and retrieval system, without permission in writing from the publisher.

Cover art: Ken Wong
Author Photo: C.J. Sage
Cover & Interior design & layout: Steven Asmussen
Copyediting: Elizabeth Nichols

Glass Lyre Press, LLC
P.O. Box 2693
Glenview, IL 60026

www.GlassLyrePress.com

CEPHALOPODIC
winner of the 2014 Kithara Book Prize

The *kithara* was an ancient Greek musical instrument in the lyre family used for solo playing, as well as to accompany poetry and song.

Previous Winners

2013 — *Idyll for a Vanishing River*, by Jeffrey C. Alfier

Contents

In Love	11
Pianist and Cypress	14
Inner Voyeur and Moon	15
New Age	17
Skydiver and Microphones	19
Cephalopodic	21
The Consumption of Time	23
Conch and Pear	24
The Rhinoceros and the Gymnast	27
Nightboat	28
Time and Time Again	29
On the Lip of the Valley	31
The Forbidden Spark	32
Blind Witness	35
The Offering of His Eye	36
Living in Italics at the Moment	37
Through the Weave	40
Bookmark	41
Tempest	43
Captured	46
Projected Leda and Swan	47
By Outward Appearances an Ox and Owl	48
Woman and Gorilla	50
A Naked Lunch	51

The Ceiling and The Floor	52
Let's Spread Ourselves	54
The Runaways	55
Love Poem With An Exaggeration of Every Little Ache	56
The Observers	57
Before the Season Truly Changes	64
Every Seven Years the Cells of the Body Are Replaced	65
Various Positions	67
Cubist Still Life	70
Late Harvest Song	71
we Dream of a House Until we Are a House	72
Within Cages	73
The Astronauts	75
Orpheus and Eurydice : Sand and Water	76
Deep Sea	77
Invisible Love Poem	78
In Love (2)	79
Acknowledgements	83
About the Author	85

In Love

The moon bares itself to a mirror
and the lake gazes lovingly back at the satellite.

He could be Daedalus the way he stares across the water.

This body of tides keeps its movements within a shoreline
while the orbiter slips closer to escape.

Lake of brush strokes and wild machinations and pullings;
lake of legs and fingering streams.

He dangles his lower limbs over the edge of stone into cooling air;
the same air that holds the sum of night,

tattooed as it is with stars, bravadoing clouds
that would riot their chests in thunder.

Night of dreamt sheep and besquirreled poplars.
Night of neck and neck and anxious branchings.

He doesn't even look her way: his head a mossy stone.
He never looks back, not for bark or grass or nuzzling clouds.

Say something!
Look curious and say it;
but what
comes out is sans serif:

"I think I hear the Dryads moaning."
Theirs is the life of roots rutting and pushing, snaking.

The tongue reveals its moss
and she is surrounded by lay-about lambs.

She dreams of combs whenever the flock is in sight.
The meadowlark goes on and on:

look at my red chest, look at my red chest—
he could learn a lot from such feathers.

Meadow of twitching ears and sea greens.
Meadow garnished with wispy curling branches.

She can hear her heart like footfalls;
she feels the impressing soleprints in her body.

Her feelings gleam like a penknife
carving their names in wrinkled bark.

She knows herself like each fraying thread
of her cutoffs.

The back of his head becomes a celestial body
but one with an elliptical orbit.

Whatcha thinking?
comes out more and less accusingly.

In this light her skin alights with the moon.
She blankets her hand over the stubble grass

where the lambs have been.
His shadow cracks the stones behind him.
She finally sighs to go down there
and shoreline with him.

As she rights herself
he turns to look long upon her.

Her eyes have their own waves
and fish and eels.

He feels his own footsteps
running the rutted paths of gravity.

Pianist and Cypress

Some days I bend over backwards just to give you the keys
of my chest, black and white—a perfect row. I don't follow music.
I am the instrument. Ears just butterfly around us. You can spread
your fingers into a web. Catch the notes out of nature.
To this end the Earth is your egg. Even I feel as though
I was hatched only moments after you tapped on my shell. I like
to dream I am a Cypress tree—always bending to get the best sun.
A view of the beach from my perch. Our shadows are young lovers
innocently cleaning the beach of the world's disposable parades.
We've both seen what people are capable of. Good and good evil.
Why can't more be like fish? Love the sea for all it is.
And then I can't help but look at you: each exquisite note you give—
emotions at the speed of sound. I spend so much time, imagining
what you look like disrobed. Like me, arms and a trunk
turning, almost knotting to catch more light.
On this cliff it is easy to see the erosion going on
all around us. I say get closer. Move a branch within
my limbs. Entangle, entwine. If the moon pulls
the water harder against rocks. If the rocks give.
We might be each others' saviors. Or we might plunge
together into the sea. I offer my broad chest of keys.
Play something no one has ever heard before.
Something to fill the emptiness above the Pacific.

Inner Voyeur and Moon

Love, I have a small confession to make:
Inside of me
the moon unravels.
There are no cathedrals only the facades of cathedrals.
The young bodies of our selves
—the ones neither of us ever knew—
embrace passion again.
Their sheets bunch and snake away
leaving them naked on the sheer edge
of a night not unlike this one
where we find ourselves now,
hand within hand.
Everything is neatly framed dishevelment—
that is to say, I'm sure
within each of those smooth bodies
another moon is unraveling
like love itself;
pulled to a final string
before respooling.
I love the way her (your)
hand opens
a gorgeous flower;
petals reflecting the lunar light.
And yes, they (we) unravel ourselves too.
We are always becoming
and undoing.
We watch ourselves
build another façade of a tombstone
out in the valley beyond
the Hollywood of our bodies.
Long shadows in the moon
like steps, like accounting
or confessing—
a measure of all the times we let go,
let the chord roll off the spool

and pool into something
new and unnamed
and just slivering into brightness
we will call ourselves.

New Age

As surely as architects fall in love
with angles and lines   I come to you

adjusting my buttons and lapel   fascinated
by the hover of your dress

as though you floated into the room
a jellyfish   a single bulb

She's not on the same field   of play
they'd all whispered to me

yet I lean forward   closer to you
and away from my secured counsel

As you speak   whole cities blossom
within my chest   a new age

out of the slow bone and flesh existence
and here ideas are   rivering through

As surely as highways pulse between
major metropolises   sex is a subtext

I imagine sliding down each ravine
and ripple   within your dress

the touch of your hand   changes
an avenue of traffic lights   to green lust

With you I dream of new equations
how y might multiply   with x
a new proof   effervescing beneath our
formalities   I don't care who's watching

I come to you wanting to build structures
together   not to gaze dumbly into your eyes

Skydiver and Microphones

First, let me address the microphones:
This is not a public affair.
When I fell out of the perfectly clear
sky it was for her.
Though you all hypothesized headlines,
I was not a bomb
or escapee. I had floated, had
drifted in love. Closed
my eyes and awakened high
above where we had lain
sleeping on our beached boat.

For the record:
I was never that close to the sun
and of flying
I still know nothing.
She slept with her hand on my chest
and I became lighter
but not a light sleeper.
In the dream I was pulled by the surf
which was her arms
and there was (is) no doubt
in trusting her lead.

As my eyes opened I could see
her lying on the deck
among the flash bulbs
eyeballs. I stiffened my body,
dove to protect her
from your gawker mob. I know
you get paid to crowd in
and record whatever you tell the curious
public to watch. How gravity pulls down
the stars like everything else
from the sky, and the laws

of physics demands its equality.
But I am no asteroid, no meteor,
nor even a comet. I rise and fall
by her side. We possess no magic
other than what anyone (even you)
holds within their bodies.
In this new hollowed crater we
shall make our bed—on the ceiling
of a cave of sleep. Safe from the news.
This statement is now over—
I have nothing more to say.

Cephalopodic

Within the body of water,
other bodies of water.
It cossets her, one tentacle

and then more.
Behind each suction cup,
a blue mark: half moon, star,

and a night sky
it only knows from rumor.
Awkwardness,

though it is governed by fluidity.
It sees farther out than she,
into tide and current, guarding.

It thinks to return her to the surface,
but with each slip across her skin,
she says, "Stay."

It cannot sleep anymore—
too many visions
of fishhooks and cleavers.

Her back curves in to it.
They are buoyant,
and it is wild-eyed:

when has it been loved like this?
It would live in her world—
bathtubbed. But she says,

"Stay here in the sea."
It wants to be her diving bell,
surround her in pocketed air,

but she will kick to the surface.
They drift in and out
of their domains,

air and water exchanges.
She moves her home to the edge.
It stays close as the surf will allow.

The Consumption of Time

He never sees her body in the faces
of clocks, nor does she see his body
in the clouds that go trouting by,
silvered as they are.

He sees her face in the housings
of clocks, the ticking of her heart
in the motion by hidden
springs and cogs.

She believes his face is the moon
or another satellite of similar size;
always able to tell time
by its phases.

Then it is not even faces
but eyes, that are themselves
miniatures of dials, of instruments,
of faces. An orbiter white as teeth

rises and sets with each lid.
She sees his mouth and only that,
lips revealing a row of planets
and a soft red bed to lie upon.

Rifts in time plank the universe—
Do you remember? she asks.
The gesso board moon rises again,
full of his lips across her sky.

Conch and Pear

A Zen garden accepts a pear
as its stone, while a conch is dangled
sharply over the sandy bed.

One sighs and a Mondrian
corner lifts and peels back.

Bed of sand, bed of calcium
and silicon, bed of mica flecks
catching the light and the sky—

blue again.

With him the sound of the sea
surrounds and curls inwardly.

He says *the world is combinations
of building blocks*;

she envisions atoms
bouncing off his shell

eventually resting upon her skin
like grains of sand.

Mirrors reflect shoulders and legs
and what has always been limitless

is suddenly served in straight angles again.

Each line and edge is a blade
slicing into the curve of her spirit.
His face in this hour: a tight spiral.

A rectangle of canvas waits
for stretching, for its color to return.

He looks into a mirror
the way she looks out a window.

She lays upon the table
and is the table—polished
to reflective perfection.

She says, *come sup*.

He is aware of the trap door
before her and walks slowly
around its cliffs.

His hands run along
her smooth finish—her corner
digging into his thigh.

She can feel his femoral pulse.
He leans into a bruise.

The sound of the surf comes
pouring into the room.

A phonograph plays warped
crooning until catching a skip
over and again the voice hiccups.

There is a sough and sand scatters
across the floor like crumbs.

Fabric catches the breeze and spills
over a border like a flag.

He furls around her shoulders
until she wears him like armor.

Her face is studied like Orphée's
mirror—looking for an opening,

a window in which to slip through
like a breath of wind.

Here the artist sleeps under her
blanket of canvas. She pulls him

down into colors, into squares,
into her quiet moment of creation.

The Rhinoceros and the Gymnast

She bends over backwards
and he shoulders the maneuver.
He does his best

to keep the horns of his head
lowered and away from her next move:
a back handspring.

Each footfall, each planted hand
wipes away the mud covering his skin—
as though she is drops of rain.

Beyond their bodies
streamers and confetti flurry.

She passes through a hoop,
he steadies his weight and walks

a plank and rope bridge;
her movement is perfection.

Her conical hat, white, is almost
 a mutant horn rising out of his back.

Her muscles defined by smudges of red dust,
still she is as bright as the moon to him.

As they move, never is heard the laughter
 of children, the moaning of the audience
 outside their spotlight.

They are not two unusual creatures
living together;
when they touch—no other thing exists.

Nightboat

She could feel the fish touching her spine
as he offered her a small torn piece of the night

it's true: she felt part of this boat, part of him
still she had carved out a space for herself

not unlike his own spot. They could not see
their own reflections on the surface

was this what coming together truly meant
instinctively, she looked at his other hand

he had pulled down a star or bright starfish—
she could not tell for sure

she held back a desire to disrobe
for him—and a fish leapt out of the water

a planet rolled off of his head
the fire in his hands gave her warmth

the harbors of his eyes never turned away

Time and Time Again

he asks, *where does the time go
when you're gone*, and builds another
house for cogs and keys

she wears a clock dial for a collar

and offers pendulums, not for the advancement of time
but to mark the subtle disturbances of his breath

he is all measurements and tools

he wears his flywheel on his sleeve
and she possesses an odd sympathy in return

he gears up to ask her something more intimate
but uncoils a mainspring at her feet

a clock face opens its eyes to mismatched arms
reaching to gather minutes and hours

his face is a glass case without a key
hers more partial to gnomon light

she feels a queer timing in her ball bearing cap
a tingle of vibration

with the click-ticking of escapement
her heart could be aflutter:
chamber of gear trains, of friction
chamber of cross beats echoing loudest

he says, *you are my remontoire*
and lets his pocket watch dangle counterclockwise
just to prove it's serious

sound of baritone bells
sound of small wooden birds

love may as well be the harbor of a harmonic oscillator
and he smiles sundial bright at her

on the hour, carved figure of a man chases
the whittled figure of woman
out one door and through another

each hour feels like seven seconds
or so she's read old news in a medical report

her pendulums feel heavier than before
what about the body's own clock?

this makes his numerals itch

the bowls of water he washed her feet in
now outflow, now another notch on his tally stick

that sounds dirty—look it up

he's all Italian hours: angles and ascensions of her constellations
she, the canonical hours: a great horologe of the giving and given

she begins to wonder, *if you do not observe or measure
does the time still float by?*
even though he thinks there is no time for this tangent
she smiles coyly

the fabric of time begins to bunch like an old curtain
she wets her finger and rings a crystal glass
and touches his accutron heart

now he sees her in a synchronous light
and whatever time is left, stops

On the Lip of the Valley

Is the woman in the shadow of want
wondering at the man
on the valley edge

Is the man looking at the patchwork
of landscape below
like it is his life

She fondles a lock of his hair
stolen from their bed
last night

The world breaks off in squares
long lines and angles

She leaves the bedroom door open
a draft rustles her summer dress

Cool air raising the fine hairs
on her thigh

His hands in the intimate spaces
of his front pockets

She imagines his hands are a soft rain
soaking her clothes to a cling

And she breathes in deep from it
tasting and smelling all of him
and she does not call him

She stays long into the shadow of want
waiting for him to turn around
accept her unspoken call

The Forbidden Spark

A chaise lounge opens itself to their bodies
and their bodies become a theater

he's projecting a romantic movie into her heart   again

he writes another love poem
the print key becomes a drawer

chest of keyboards, and worn letters
chest of shift keys and directions

much of the afternoon is spent drinking wine
with bread and chocolate

her torso turns and repositions
leaning closer to him

he tries to focus on her voice, but the window light
accentuating her curves will have none of that

his compass spins and spirals
hers turns ouroboric

he follows her thigh
to its locked conclusion
he beams more celluloid dreams

somewhere else someone reads his poem
and becomes a chaise lounge

what begins with a sprocketing noise inside his chest
reels upward to the chambered lamp
images ray forward as the film rubs and passes
and spools in his mind

color of wine and upholstery
color of silver screen and chroma key

wood grains of the floorboards spell out equations
the wallpaper patterns itself after circuit boards

a spark of electricity makes the long journey
around the room

she sings, *what's wrong with a good musical?*

Gene Kelly is lonely in unrequited love again
waiting for his happy ending

as the first apes are eating their apple
lost in the sweetness of taste

somewhere else other readers have turned a page

she holds a note like a pheromone
he feels other gears, other sprockets whir

he motions one finger *to come*
and their bodies get a little closer now

her collar bone forms a heart shape
at the base of her neck
he notes her pulse

and matches it with the speed of his movie
one long, slow kiss projected onto her heart

there is a surge of energy
between them

he points to his favorite scene upon her chest
and she touches his extended finger

completing the circuit

Blind Witness

if I leave my eyes closed
the trees become blind witnesses

and the eyeball moon
keeps to itself as it passes

the lark does not sing, nor the nightingale

she rests on my chest
and I feel each breath she takes

beneath our tree stump bed
the sound of termites propagating

I hum a slight tune between
each rise and fall of her

something that will haunt her mind
in the waking hours

were you singing this and she hums it back
then I close my eyes to return

to our night bed

The Offering of His Eye

Across the dinner table
He offers his eye
She pulls a magnifying glass
As he holds her hair
And dreams pillows of her scent
The curtains ghost and flap
Lightning in the distance
Drops stick figures to the ground
—Rigid and stiff
He can feel static air building in the room
Three rain drops fill his palm
A partial answer to a farm prayer
He listens to her steady breathing
Like counting thunder
Their shadows grow from the raw bulb above
Blending on the swirling eddies of wood grain
Her skin was smooth
He can sense this through her movements
The rustle of her clothes
He holds onto her hair long after
She's done looking into his eye

LIVING IN ITALICS AT THE MOMENT
—Melissa Stein

a font is open to the idea of slanting
and slanting bends itself to a curl

summer through an open window

offers new acoustics to the room
he presses against her back as if to pose

she is inclined to this line of thinking
whisper something, she requests

put something out there—risk yourself

he tilts his head slightly to one side
inquisitive, but her expression is one of waiting

there are rumors of fluidity
water surely, but sap, and tar, and molasses, too

his face is taijituic
hers is wood grain and crosshatched fabric

her lines, the plume of her dress,
ruffles and pleats conspire
to a camber

the light of the chamber has its own attitude
a bias, shadow and predisposition

this does not stop his hand from reaching
her shoulder

he is the very crest and wave of a string bass
while hers is linen and spindrift

the music is that hushed thump against cloth
like wind through broken sails

a scarf drapes over stone
the crack in the floor is nearly a perfect angle

walls meet but in odd degrees

she whispers, *pitch*
he suggests, *roll*

the tune of the room lowers its volume
even though there are swishes of caress

what burns beneath their breastplates
are aspirant desires

in outward appearances
there is courtly bowing and formality

although a secret nod
a shared twinkling wink of the eyes

a note passed in palms
the cursive slant of it all

she is all pins and needles with his touch

the ruffle of her cuffs lends her arm
to a stamen lean from an iris

the strange garden of this gradient light
she feels one of her garments turn to water

cloth quickly pools at their feet
revealing the polish of their skin

the door creaks closed
to their quiet recline

Through the Weave

There is no room, no molded corners, no blue walls
textured like water. There is no skin deep, or skin
for that matter. We kiss where our shrouds touch,
and without distraction of light or color, I am left
to the subtle pleating of fabric. Your ghost
coming through the weave of threads, and I
cannot remember the features of your face
as much as the smoothness or your cheek, your chin.
We are not living in darkness as much as gauzy fog.
Here the braille of you is the only language
I need on my lips. Above our heads the air grows
unstable, electric—my fingers find your arm's
goose flesh. It is easy to believe there is no one
left in the world. That beyond our curtains,
our mists and smoke, a silent sea settles
over the planet—and we are set adrift
in the slow currents of our pulse.
There is no room around us, no molded corners,
no walls to shelter or block us.

Bookmark

with a line from May Sarton

She sits reading at the end
of his long body.

She believes
all secrets reveal themselves

in the study of a falcon.
She notes this in the margins.

Naked in the sun, he reads
from a book planted above his groin.

He reclines like a guest on her
snowy chaise—the back frames him

like a halo. She studies the plumped
chest of the bird, its head moving

to each stimulation of sound and sight.
He mouths the words from the page

Better to stare the senseless wind...
she barely reveals a smile.

The dog waits to be noticed,
watching her pencil scratching, she turns

a page, the falcon rises and swoops.
It would nuzzle the man's drooped hand,

but prefers a patient reward.
The hips and thighs of the hills

are the hawk's distraction,
its always hunting its next lunch—

the turning of another page, her pencil
undulating do not pretend to be mice.

He wriggles his fingers and the dog
moves in for a rub. He twitches his toes

and she makes another note.
Disinterested, the falcon moves on.

In these tight shadow hours
love might be the speck of a bird,

the floppy ears of a setter,
the shade within the crook of a book—

a scribble in the margins,
and a delicate bookmark for return.

Tempest

1.

We pretend to understand
the weather
to this end we take the wind
into our chests
pearls of clouds
roll
off of our lips
and thunderheads
crowd the peaks
of our living room chairs
your face
looks downward
with waning interest
at the herds
of white tuffs

the winds catch
the body of curtains
the body of your skirt
your hair
in this moment
I see you as a god
with your collar
of clouds

2.

Did I hear you just then
saying you'd lassoed clouds
and left them hanging out to dry

and ghost away
to nothing—in your slow,
diminishing wonder?

*It's not a science
until you've broken them down
and rebuilt them, repeatedly.*

You study my face—
it makes my barometer spin
frenzied and crazy.

3.

I spin the world for you
and you pick a spot

that makes weathermen say,
freak storm, unusual front.

Within me an ocean steams
you say you can teach me

the cycle of water. I open my mouth
and cumuli escape.

I have no want for knowledge—
I tell you I'm a tactile learner.

Yours is a lesson plan smile,
and enough heat

to overcast a hemisphere
for well over a year.

4.

Do you ever remember the life you lived before this one?

Even the short years and months prior?

Another cloud unravels itself before us—

None of it ever seems *real*—

I dreamt of sheet music roiling into clouds again.

A breeze whistles through the reeds I call thoughts.

Unholster your woodwind, love.

To your wry smile I feel my face turning white and moist.

I feel myself pulled to the currents of your Tropic of Cancer—

cyclones along the coastlines, more heat in the ocean,

my eye a storm focusing in the kinetic latitudes.

Captured

She says this is how we define ourselves in love
and continues her brushstroke

across the dimples of canvas I am naked
in a pose she has chosen for me

the floor suggests a giant chessboard
but we are not at war nor is this a game

I continue to hold still, though I am a big mouth
and the note held in my throat

begins to swan-neck, to stretch an S
up to my tongue

the rippling curtains full of color
transform that side of the room into a jungle

where I might come out with a thousand creatures
to offer my competitive love song

I am all brass and stainless steel in my delivery
—something Miles, something Coltrane, something Bird—

proud among the wild roars and screeches—
a primal horn and reed

she says perfect
and leans closer for a clearer perspective

Projected Leda and Swan

Within the shrouds of ourselves the riveted and patched
swan seeks out the shelter of her polished wood grains.
She reaches for a marbled seed to feed the nicked black beak.
His body wants to become a lyre or a lute—
something as hollow as he is, but resonate, soundful,
a sonorous joy to her.
She holds a coy pose of herself,
as though a camera will shutter an image of her.

Our projected selves remember our lives in different truth—
as gods. In this way, we move
into better poses and close our eyes.
The colors we witness intensify.
The holy order of our robes begins to cling and sway.
I will admit the want of my animus to S
near your shoulder as you offer a sanded glance back.
Dearest, we seem most finished at our extensions.

Here, yes, I give a slight flap of my riveted wings
and dip my head in to nuzzle your waist.
Squared and hinged, dimpled and rusted,
I reflect the clouded light in rigid certainty.
Love, ignore the limits placed on form and the angled
beginnings and endings in other peoples' eyes—
I've flown for you.
Changed into the best swan I could make

from memory. Let me slip under your arm.
And in this way, we touch. Like smooth surfaces,
like the roll of my chest against hers. Like silk
and feather. I pin the rough edges of my wings back—

an intimate strategy. A singing tuning fork of a pry-bark.
Take me apart, Love, one rivet, one nail, one screw
at a time. This is not violence I implore, this is nothing
but the revealing I was too scared to wished for.

By Outward Appearances an Ox and Owl

A stump mimics another stump
until slowly the forest recedes

weathered branches have their own acoustics

she lowers her face a little
and he pulls his snout down

dress of feathers and intricate camouflage
dress of false eyes and misdirection

the starless sky rests on bare arms
and the goosebumps become their own stars

their masks stare holes into space
the sight of gravity, the gravity of eyes

he counts the rings of the stump she rests upon
she imagines the bark of his torso

his face: a question mark
hers: heart-shaped

with her eyes, she follows the curve
of his parenthetical horns
dreaming the italics
she might hide inside them

Girl, I've got a pocket full of moths

she watches wings wriggle and whisper
from his furry coat
he imagines the sound of fur and feather
touching, the first rain of the season
distant thunder, her chest against his ear

both are a welling, a rising, a feeling
of moths in the moonless night

scuttle of leaves in the drying grass
makes this rendezvous more secret

—hush of breeze and the spiraling

she is framed by a tree with lovers initials
carved in, expanded with the growing trunk

as though this spot has always been
a separate place for expression

what light comes is no heavenly body
but earthly and delightful in the eye

the lowering of the facades
all the while not taking an eye off each other

not a blink nor glance beyond
just the fragile miracle of *now*

I love your wildflower mind

the clearing becomes a room
a chamber of the heart in the woods

they will come here on the darkest nights
to offer up to the sky

the planets, the suns spun from their love

Woman and Gorilla

Only he can hold a bunch of flowers
Like a punch in the face.
She puts one foot upon the corner
As if to back flip or dive off the edge—
His other massive paw hammocks her.
She sets free the ribbons in her hair
And he watches each like an omen.
This moment has its own gravity
—in another movie, he would carry her
Away, a shiny possession, passion
Played out against heroic men;
But he feels her touch upon his skin
And does not wonder how she could
Love him. She never speaks of human
Animals she has loved—true apes in
Wife-beaters, drunk or broken
By some rumbling in their chests.
She looks into his eyes
And there is no need for questions,
No use for language. There is trust.
When she opens her robe like a pea pod
splitting—the halo light surrounding them
becomes the only place he does not see red.

A Naked Lunch

It was getting close to straight up noon

He was dreaming a bridge

To straddle the bay's quietude

She moved an arm under his

The picnic cloth bunched

Beneath and bramble between them

With their shadows they made

Other couples

Limbs snaked and twined

Their hair pretended to be sheets

Her mind was on rolling hills

Both were rapt and rewrapped

Boulders rolled to the valleys

Like beads of sweat

Sweet fruit grew softer in the heat

They spread out the cloth back out

Like so much spilt milk

The Ceiling and The Floor

they live in a hall of mirrors
where neither one reflects

she spends most of her time on the ceiling
he walks the barefoot floors
finding sheet music like tiles

in the afternoons she plays piano
one slow steady note follows another
reverberating off glass

he sits on a hard chair listening to the hours
of her fingering voice—never looking up

outside the weather has its way with the world
sometimes a sound enters the room
like a mouse

his thoughts: quicksilver beading and rolling
hers: calluses over nerve endings

from her perspective: he sits on the ceiling
watching each sheet she floats to him

she wants to see his face
tilt to hers

she taps the pedal with her foot
"the body is its own instrument"

but comes alive in the accompaniment of others

hours of minutia in wordplay
god, I love you when you're angry

she looks at his face inquisitively
sadly framed by an intellectual brow

"you're too damn smart
for your own good"

hands clasp around a raised knee
he knows the next note she'll play

all the blood rushes to her head
the world has turned upside down

four walls to keep them in—both
incomplete without an opposing face

Let's Spread Ourselves

like a catch dumped out
from a fishing net onto a deck.
Love, I am a wave crashed
over you. Spilling arms, legs,
ribs over your arms, legs,
ribs. Let's not waste our time
talking about diving helmets,
slickers, and neoprene gloves.
Let the ropes and the hoses
snake and eel across the deck,
across our bodies seeking
escape and redemption.
I don't care how their drama plays
out—leave them to their hiss-
choiring fates. Let's run our fingers
through the currents of hair,
over our salt valleys and hills.
The wave of my tongue crashes
the shore of your lips. Let's fishtail
ourselves, flop if we must! Let's be
the catch of the day, the record
haul, the bountiful. Love, let's call
ourselves *the first catch*, Eve
and her Adam, each one half
of the other's apple.

The Runaways

I rest you on a sandy star

outlined in cyan—

you, painted blue.

I am a red shifted jester,

it's true. But looking at you, here,

with the uproarious circus around us;

fisticuff clowns jousting candy canes;

Love, you are the only logical thing.

The audience of arched eyebrows

and laughter cannot see us

beneath all this horseplay.

Kiss me, face-paint appearances be damned!

We were kids when we joined the slapstick

big top life, tonight let's lift the tent's veil

and run away before the final show.

Love Poem with An Exaggeration of Every Little Ache

It begins with the breaking body
of clouds, crumbling into smaller,
less recognizable parts.

As your hand drifts away, settles
on the ground, I offer you an apple
and pretend, Oh Love, we are not

Eve and Adam. My feet fall away
and I run a finger along the rough
edges of our phantom limbs.

I take you into my arms, resting
your head against my shoulder so
you might watch the red moon rise.

Love, I can no longer tell what is
stone and what are our break-aways.
I feel you press into me—risking the dust.

The Observers

Everything is reduced to measurements of waiting

                small grains of sand spiral and sift

      downward, each a moment following a moment following...

Don't stare at the counting! It slows the world!

          And I think of you in my arms

                    if we just watched the clock ticking

            how much longer we would have together

                even if it is merely   the act of observing
something else

                          *

what if we wake up from a trance of time

                      to discover a stone shell

surrounds our embrace—   as though we had survived   Pompeii?

Around us

   other couples equally waking from a hypnosis of clocks

      uncertain of the landscape or the constellations

the stretch and yawn of geometric periods

     shaking free from our skin.

*

   Stunned we can see there is still sand in the chamber—

plenty of time left on the clock.

    And how could we not wake up stronger: nearly invincible?

  Each grain, each tic, a unit of patience;

there had never been value in a rushing life

        or a harness—too many times had we been

described as an engine   or a spinning part of an engine.

        *

Is it the act of observing or loving,

        or the art of lovingly observing

that mires time? Yet we do not notice

        any diminished movement of our own

even the chambers of our hearts

        must flood and empty

by some measurement

        one more beat to prove my point.

*

We do not   see time itself

    yes, the effects; yes, the counting;

the audible pace of a metronome, a cog, a drum beat;

    the throb of sun yellowing the page;

the erosion of coastlines—

        even the rock that shelled us

    breaks into grains of sand

            enough to fill the hourglass we
deny—

*

a beach of hour glasses

        the roar and hiss of every wave— another measurement

if you really wish to count them

        instead of enjoying the unique curl and color of each

was that a school of fish within the body

        of one? Another with dolphin?

Then spindrift?

        Each glass chamber has its own imperfections:

wave or warp; a bubble of air.

        Each grain the surface of a planet—

molecules and atoms in a slightly different dance.

*

So many things to observe!

    Or should I spend this moment

running my hand along your forearm

        observe your reaction

start a chain reaction

    the sough of your breath, the exhale

nearly the sound   of sand slipping through glass.

*

Who cares where

    the time goes   unseen like a back fence cat

sleek against the broad leaves, gold-eyed and watching

    our abandon.   Who wants to stop time

just to watch an accountant ring another tic into his registry

      some animals give their lives   to have one pure moment

of loving.

                      One pure sensual moment with their eyes closed.

Before the Season Truly Changes

How electric the body in this closeness
we've grown into. Our heads together

in a kiss, a canopy; branches of nests
and a hive of bees—honeycombs to hold

all our feelings. A small drone of desire
is released—a quantum dance

before buzzing into the immediate
air. Whisper of bark against bark,

whisper of branching out—the long stretch
before another seasonal change.

I love to look at you in this new Autumn light:
to touch your roots, your knots, your last leaves

just before they fall.

Every Seven Years the Cells of the Body are Replaced

Although I can feel my body crumble   fall away
my spine is anchored   to a bolt in the floor

to this end   I am her eternal partner
sitting opposite to her   holding the points of her feet

assisting her stretch   she sighs
once I was a beautiful dancer   and my skin is as cold as the moon

why I feel such guilt   I do not know
her knee damaged long before   I ever   knew her

perhaps it is that I was not there
to watch her *own* a floor
hypnotize an audience

we are so many things
in our lives
the dust of my former self
accumulates into a new
arrangement

to this end   she watches me
with a ready hand

she too is changing   cells and perceptions
slough away   to dust

the parts of us that love
grow and replace   not love   but the house of love

those open doors   that place
where we understand   each other's changes

where even in the darkest corners
we embrace the concrete   and flesh

of what we have been
and are about to become

Various Positions

1.

It was always nearing midnight;
it was the listening to the other breath
into the mouthpiece;
she was already primping her mind
with rollers, what make-up would go
with a new dress.
He would fill the space between
her breathing with a selection of baubles;
all-the-while naked
his body waiting like raw fuel.
She could sit in the twilight
of appliance lights
for an eternity;
he was on the line
sharing the little things of a day.
She would not move
—muscles cramping—
not wanting to ruin the moment.

2.

In the Sunday afternoons of their love
they would occupy a room
with various hobbies
and a dog they called their *child*.
Both dressed to go out
though they rarely did.
The loveseat genuflected;
the lamp swayed;
and the family portraits kept
their empty, simian vigils.

A gnat nagged his face
to angry retaliation—
No dear, it isn't you!
But some things cannot be unreleased;
thunder rattled the windows,
rain stained beautiful patterns
on the wall—some appeared as flowers
others the visions of patient gods.

3.

On those unemployed evenings
unexplainable politics crept in.
She offered him the classifieds
but he passed them by
for another issue of *The Panderers' Parade*
or to dream himself a funny page superhero.
She was naked, her breast at eye-level
but he never stopped reading.
She saw past the dirty underwear
to the man she knew
was still in there,
she pushed greasy hair
off his forehead and watched him reading—
his chest a steady rhythm.
She ran into the bedroom
laid on her stomach, legs scissoring
the air behind her
twirling the phone chord in her finger
listening to him breath into the mouthpiece
again.

4.

In the quiet hours of reflective morning light
they are in love again—
wandering, hand in hand, through
the rooms of their home.
Each door the entry into a new age
or period in the fossil record—
a full journey
like the turn and twist
of a telephone wire.
She said, *let my ear be your mouthpiece—*
breathe for me.
The bed knelt down before them
and they fell in.
To each other's ears:
a whisper of private language—
the inward spiral
of cartilage and skin,
the drum, the hammer, the anvil;
the reawakening to desire.

Cubist Still Life

There are times when I am only the negative
space where an apple had been;

when everything about her says fruit.
Do not confuse my envy with hunger.

When I touch her there is a scent of apples
and oranges mingling.

In a small chamber where shadows
play with our figures

my head becomes a bowl of earth.
When I look in her eyes citrus seeds

sprout and take root.

When I listen to her heart, one Red
Delicious whispers

its song into bloom.

Late Harvest Song

It was getting well into the harvest;

time was the rainbow trout in his head.

She plucked the onion of her lute,

he strummed the lemon strings,

and both of them

became a meal.

Her face was a sunny yoke

delicately centered

in her collar of bread.

The autumn light lifted

the humidity of a previous season.

He sang of breakfast

and she of dinner.

Neither wishing to sleep or dream

but fill the other's mouth.

She and he wished only to nourish

while all around them

the grapes realized their wine.

WE DREAM OF A HOUSE UNTIL WE ARE A HOUSE

we dream of a house   until we are a house
    sleeping head to head
on a bed
        of blueprints and layouts
on a bed
        of permits filed
                  and stamped *APPROVED*
on a bed
        of ourselves expressed
            by walls and rooms
                      the pitch and angled roof
the architect's signature on a sheet
              across our chests
wire schematics spider
            within our skin—veins of light,
the ducts   of ourselves
         the crawlspaces,
the places   where we will learn
              what courses within
              the walls
              and beneath
              the floorboards
our bodies   form a foundation
         arms around the other's head
here a wall goes up
         until we are safe
within.

Within Cages

Within their cages they are their cages;
fingers wrapped around bars
she stares at the back of his head.

He sits at the piano and attempts
a prison tune,
notes obscured by sweating metal.

The potted flowers watch
as winter rages outside
from the safety of their jails

no petal ventures beyond
the slotted air. Even the peacock
walks with a gilded coop around him—

plume touching wire top.
The man looks into the piano
and sees the strings as slats,

as are the legs, the black keys,
the floor boards, the pleated
curtains—this house built

to hold all of his loves. She too
has worked the hours of welding
slots and squeaking hinges

that cry out like alarmed
peacocks. In the quiet light
that does not fill a room

but casts angular shadows
upon the furniture she wears
a map of the world

for a dress, but her hands
never touch a continent
nor an island.

She remembers her own skin
against his, and to this end
their clothes have become corrals.

In his mind, he is playing
what Orpheus might have plucked:
his love for her in notes

and each caress of a key
is how he would touch her.
They, even in these cages

are always close, never seen
without the other near.
He knows she is behind him

senses her fingers stretching
to him, and leans back to brush
her body, lifts a locked-up hand

to reach rearward. One clank
of metal against metal is all
he needs to tell him she is

there following his music, his body—
he wants to turn around but
but does not risk losing her.

The Astronauts

How many times had he taken her to the moon?
What he remembers are her red boots
contrasted against white dust—
each footprint an invitation to follow her home.
He remembers the first time her auburn hair
caught the wind of liftoff—
a new flag to pledge his allegiance.
They both could not wait
to romp the white craters;
to ride out to the Sea of Tranquility
and make out in the lunar rover.

Now in these cutback years,
this Age of Scrapped Missions,
his breath pushes through her hair—
a quiet ripple of their stars and stripes;
forever a reminder of their places
in the galaxy.

Orpheus and Eurydice: Sand and Water

Because I still love you I will play anything
to make the sea bring you closer to me;
to give the angry gods a little peace
here, at the shore, I stroke your hair
that comes in wave after wave.
Naked, I wade into the surf
reaching across the crests,
so cold I have forgotten my body—
Love, I am nearly a ghost
trying to touch you—nearly a ghost
in the waters where we both ran
stopping to pluck uninteresting shells.
I swim the torrents, arming further
out to you—the rhythm of the ocean
is a frenzied breathing, gasping air,
one hand before the other, senseless
legs paddling into the swirling currents
like your hair. I lost myself years ago
out here in the surf of your body;
I am only a song, a ghost song,
whispered as water pulls back
through sand, the intense orchestra
that draws the spirit closer, closer
to come and become
again and again.

Deep Sea

Mostly, I am adrift—
arms and legs in slow akimbo;
I look into watery light.
Your hand kelps to touch
the blue fish of my heart.
Now an ocean pounds
the coastline of my chest.
There are fins
in the space between us.
You swim beneath
and around me—
seagrass hair brushing
my skin to tingles.
When I look into the seas
of your eyes, the fish within
my body muscle
and shimmy. I do
not love you
because you saved me,
it is the abyss
within your eyes
that offers all the water
to the world
but will not let me drown.

Invisible Love Poem

She thinks about the aubade she writes upon his back each morning; how he walks through each day with a poem he nor anyone else can see. And some mornings after it is written on his skin, she sits and reads the lines over and over again, like morning prayer, like *dear god, please watch over this man—keep him safe*, only it is not a plea, it is her heart in words behind his. She worries about the day ahead, after they shower and dress and part from each other for the mundane tasks that make a paycheck, that mean food and rent. Sometimes the lines are asking why the world is made so, why they must get up at least five days out of the week to be bored or feel trapped in a cubical cage. Now she touches him lightly enough as not to wake him yet. She remembers how, last night, what seems only moments, on this bed, they fell into each other's embrace, and the world shrunk to just the room, and their warmth was the only heat needed. She is counting the seconds now, before the alarm clock goes off; over and over again in her mind: *should I turn it off so we can stay here together, be each other's nourishment and shelter; or risk the new day?*

In Love (2)

Still years later and the moon looks long upon the bed
of mock stars lining the shore.

The reflected orb scatters like Icarus' feathers upon the waves.

Their bodies are the only shepherds of movement
as we watch the satellite escape to the horizon.

Within their sleep the clouds came down to us as sheep;
our own kids—oily as dreams.

He curls up next to a ewe and makes a pillow of her;
breathing in the scent of night grass,

wildflowers closed for the evening still offering a slight fragrance
of the business of daylight.

Here in their sleep, the sheep watch over them,
Here in their sleep their bodies are youth remembered.

She is the limb of a cypress, stretching toward him.
She feels energy drawn up from the earth.

Nothing is said.
Both twitch in their dreams;
both feel
the serifs of roots:

"You look like a Dryad, Dear."
Theirs has been a life of soil and branching.

A mouth opens to knot-hole music.
He gathers the clouds of sheep to huddle and listen.

He combs through their lanolin comfort;
an owl's song from the branches:

Who, who knew? Who, who knew?—
but rarely is anything gained from the answer.

Bed of roots and subtle creaks.
Bed of grass and soft bleats.

Within his body, her bare feet pad green paths;
a sound he carries—has never been without.

His fingers run over the old carvings:
their names in an equation.

Not as bright as first carved so many years before,
but a comfort to the touch.

She has always been his earth,
his orbit well-timed and tabled.

I knew you'd like this—
he gives her a stone polished by the river.

He slips his hand into hers.
His other hand a blanket for the union:

a flock of fingers to watch over.
Once, he owned a powerful shadow, but not in her light.

He has come to rest her by her feet
in both the dream and the dreamt reality.

She will wake to find him there
again and again.
His body twitching as the sheep do
in their sleep.

She hears her own footsteps
in every breath he takes in.

Acknowledgements

The author wishes to thank the editors and the staff of the following magazines where the poems first appeared:

A-minor
    The Astronauts

Atticus Review
    Inner Voyeur and Moon

Burning Bush
    Let's Spread Ourselves

The Collagist
    Every Seven Years the Cells of the Body are Replaced

Diode
    Cephalopodic

iO
    The Rhinoceros and the Gymnast

International Han Language Poetry (in English and Chinese)
    In Love
    In Love (2)
    Within Cages

Linebreak
    New Age

Mipoesias
    Love Poem with An Exageration of Every Little Ache
    Orpheus and Eurydice: Sand and Water

Phren-Z
    Captured

POET'S MARKET (2014)
    The Offering of His Eyes

RED WHEELBARROW
    Through the Weave

REDACTIONS
    Woman and Gorilla

THE SMOKING POET
    The Consumption of Time

SCAPEGOAT REVIEW
    Bookmark

SCYTHE
    Love as Pianist and Cypress

SOUNDZINE
    living in italics at the moment

uCITY REVIEW
    Conch and Pear (originally published as "Love as Conch and Pear")

VERDAD
    On the Lip of the Valley

The author also wishes to thank his wife, CJ Sage, for all the support, suggestions and, of course, love— without her the author would not have been able to write such a book. The author also wishes to thank the members of The Workshop of the Ekphrastic Bard where some of the poems were first offered.

The author offers his gratitude to Ken Wong for the cover art which was part of the inspiration for the title poem. And finally, the author is thankful to Ami Kaye, Mark McKay and Steven M. Asmussen, the amazing staff of Glass Lyre Press.

About the Author

J.P. Dancing Bear is the author of thirteen other collections of poetry. His work has appeared in *American Literary Review, Crazyhorse, Shenandoah* and elsewhere. His honors include the 2002 Slipstream Chapbook Prize, the 2010 PEN Oakland-Josephine Miles National Literary Award, Highly Commended in The Forward Prize 2010 (UK), and 15 Pushcart nominations. He is the founding editor of *The American Poetry Journal*, and owner of Dream Horse Press, publisher of the Orphic Prize and APJ Book Prize series, as well as the first animal rights poetry anthology *And We The Creatures*. He is the host of "Out of Our Minds" a weekly radio show for public radio station KKUP featuring some of today's best contemporary poets.

Glass Lyre Press

exceptional works to replenish the spirit

Glass Lyre Press is an independent literary publisher interested in technically accomplished, stylistically distinct, and original work. Glass Lyre seeks diverse writers that possess a dynamic aesthetic, and an ability to emotionally and intellectually engage a wide audience of readers.

Glass Lyre's vision is to connect the world through language and art. We hope to expand the scope of poetry and short fiction for the general reader through exceptionally well-written books, which evoke emotion, provide insight, and resonate with the human spirit.

Poetry Collections
Poetry Chapbooks
Select Short & Flash Fiction
Anthologies

www.GlassLyrePress.com

www.ingramcontent.com/pod-product-compliance
Lightning Source LLC
Chambersburg PA
CBHW021447080526
44588CB00009B/736